Witches,
Pumpkins,
and Grinning Ghosts

WITCHES, PUMPKINS, and GRINNING GHOSTS

The Story of the Halloween Symbols

by EDNA BARTH

illustrated by URSULA ARNDT

THE SEABURY PRESS • NEW YORK

ACKNOWLEDGMENT

The stanza on page 70 is from "Halloween Indignation
Meeting," copyright © 1963 by Margaret Fishback Antolini.
It appears in *Poems Made Up to Take Out,* published
by David McKay Company, Inc., and is reprinted by
permission of the publisher.

Text copyright © 1972 by Edna Barth
Illustrations copyright © 1972 by Ursula Arndt
Library of Congress Catalog Card Number: 72-75705
ISBN: 0-8164-3087-X

Designed by Carol Basen
Printed in the United States of America

Contents

*T*he night of *October 31* is a time of ghosts and goblins, devils and demons, Jack-O'-Lanterns, witches, and cats. It is a night of bobbing for apples, telling fortunes, and listening to ghost stories.

At Halloween it is fun to look frightening and to be pleasantly frightened yourself. You know it is make-believe. But the leering devils, the grinning Jack-O'-Lanterns, the cackling witches, and all the other Halloween symbols go back to a time when people, young and old, lived in real dread of goblins and ghosts, of witches and cats—especially at Halloween.

7

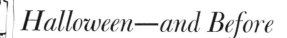

Halloween—and Before

The Celtic people, who lived more than two thousand years ago in what are now France and the British Isles, feared the evening of October 31 more than any other of the year. It was the eve of their festival of *Samhain*, Lord of the Dead. Evil spirits were everywhere.

In order to please Samhain, the Celtic priests, known as Druids, held cruel fire rites. Prisoners of war, criminals, or animals were burned alive in weirdly shaped baskets. By observing the way they died, the Druids saw omens of the future, good and bad.

Charms, spells, and predictions of the future were believed to have more power on the eve of Samhain, when so many spirits were abroad. For if due honor was paid them, the spirits might help with the magic. If ignored, they might hinder or punish the person performing it.

8

Samhain was a joyful harvest festival as well as a day of the dead. It marked the death of the old year and the beginning of a new one. The day itself was a time for paying honor to the sun god Baal, who had given the ripened grain, now safely stored away.

In the first century before Christ, Roman armies invaded Britain and Gaul, as France was called, and made them part of the Roman Empire. Many Roman soldiers stayed on in the new territories.

The Romans had a festival for the dead in late October, the *Feralia.* In November they honored Pomona, goddess of orchards. The two festivals gradually blended with the Druid Samhain. Some of the Roman soldiers adopted the beliefs of the Druids, and there were Druid converts in Rome itself.

This disturbed the Roman emperors, and they banned the Druid religion. The Druid priests were hunted down and many were killed. Those who escaped went into hiding.

9

But though their priests were gone, the Celts held firmly to their Druid customs. Year after year, on the eve of Samhain, they built bonfires and prepared for the arrival of spirits.

In the meantime, a new religion, Christianity, had been born. Weak at first, with few followers, it grew until, in the fourth century after Christ, the Roman Emperor Constantine declared it lawful. In all parts of the Roman Empire, the Christian fathers did their utmost to stamp out everything *pagan,* as they branded the older religions.

It was hard to persuade the conquered Celts that the gods they had known for centuries were evil. It was harder still to wipe out their rites and symbols. So the Christian church gave them new meanings and new names.

Celtic people who became Christians were told that the fire rites they had held for the Lord of the Dead on October 31 would now protect them against the Devil—the enemy of God and the Christian church.

In the seventh century, the church set
aside *All Saints' Day* in memory of early Christians who died for their beliefs. All Saints' Day
was first celebrated in May, but by the year
900 the date had been changed to November 1.

Within the church the festival for the pagan Lord of the Dead had become a festival of
Christian dead. In people's homes the ghostly
spirits of the older holiday lingered on.

The Celtic people who became the
Scotch, Irish, and English went on expecting
the arrival of ghosts on October 31. Gathering
in groups, they trembled at unusual sounds
and shuddered at stories of ghosts met in pre-
vious years.

But, in the tradition of the ancient Samhain harvest celebration, they also enjoyed themselves, feasting on nuts and apples, telling fortunes, dancing, and playing games.

Another name for All Saints' Day was *All Hallows*. October 31 was known as *All Hallows' Even*, which was later shortened to *Halloween*.

In the tenth century, November 2 was set aside by the church as *All Souls' Day* in memory of the souls of *all* the dead.

Halloween, All Saints' Day, and All Souls' Day come so close together and have so much in common that in some countries they tend to merge.

For people of France, southern Europe, and Latin America, it is still mainly a religious season.

In the United States, some Christians observe All Saints' Day or All Souls' Day, or both. Halloween stands on its own. It was brought here in the nineteenth century by the Scotch and Irish. And with it came the Halloween witch and cat, the devils and demons, the goblins and ghouls.

12

The Goblins Will Get You!

Ugly, menacing little creatures, believed to live underground or in dark places, goblins followed a strange path into Halloween. Like banshees, leprechauns, brownies, or pixies, they stand for the evil spirits that were once thought to emerge at Samhain and later on the eve of All Saints' Day, or Halloween.

These creatures were also known as the *Little People*, or fairy folk. In different places, the fairy folk had different names. The French called them goblins. As All Saints' Day approached, French children were warned, "The goblins will get you if you don't watch out!"

13

Where did these fairy folk come from?
Were they simply something that people made
up?

Not exactly. During the Stone Age, a
small, darkskinned people lived in northern
Europe and the British Isles. In Britain they
were conquered by the Celtic invaders, in
northern Europe, by Germanic tribes.

The dwarf people of Britain averaged
four and one-half feet in height. They lived
in forests or in hiding near forts and towns.
Their low huts, roofed with turf, looked much
like mounds. The green clothing they wore
blended with the fields and forests. This helped
to protect them from the conquerors, who con-
tinually hunted and persecuted them.

Never risking open attack on their ene-
mies, the dwarf people waylaid travelers, kid-
napped, and sometimes murdered. The little
stone arrows they shot at people and cattle
were known as elf bolts.

Now and then someone would catch a
glimpse of the Little People, and be amazed
at the way they vanished, as if by magic. Their
secretive ways, swiftness, and unusual size convinced the Celts that they were fairies and,
therefore, evil.

15

Many a housewife put out dishes of food for the dwarf people at night, hoping to keep them from harming her home and family. Any food that was left in the morning was thrown away in case the little people had poisoned it. For they were said to deal in poisons as well as magic.

Nothing is known of the religion of these dwarf people except that once every seven years they made a human sacrifice to their god. For this purpose they stole children from their neighbors, the Celts.

Whatever their religion, they despised the church bells that stood for the god of their hated neighbors.

The Little People also hated their enemy's superior iron tools. Their own tools were crude ones, made of stone.

Legends and stories tell of mortals who married fairies. This could mean that, in time, the Little People were absorbed by the Celts around them.

Whether they really were absorbed or just died out, stories about the Little People were handed down. Gradually, through the centuries, the real dwarf people were trans-

16

formed into elves, goblins, and other fairy folk.

The grassy roofs of their low houses became the fairy mounds, the green of their clothing the color for fairy clothes. Their custom of dancing in a circle became the fairy circle.

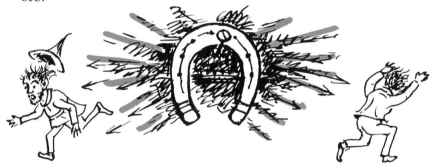

The iron the Little People had feared and hated became a protective charm. Touching iron or hanging it above a doorway was said to scare the fairies away and bring good luck. An iron horseshoe was especially lucky because of its crescent shape, once sacred to a pagan moon goddess.

The church bells so feared by the little Stone Age people rang loudly on Halloween to keep fairies at bay.

If milk spilled or cream soured, the fairy folk were usually blamed, especially around Halloween.

17

By then, fairies and goblins of various kinds and with various names had taken the place of the spirits of the dead of early Samhain festivals. They were all symbols of danger and evil, and greatly feared at Halloween.

> Hallowe'en will come, will come.
> Witchcraft will be set agoing.
> Fairies will be at full speed,
> Running in every pass.
> Avoid the road, children, children.

The storybook fairy, a tiny creature with gauzy wings, has little resemblance to the goblins and other beings once known by that name. But goblins continue, as much a part of Halloween as witches, pumpkins, or cats.

The Halloween Witch

With her black cloak and peaked hat,
her broomstick and cat, the witch is
the central symbol of Halloween, and the one
with the strangest history. Her name comes
from the Saxon word *wica,* meaning wise one.

THE WITCH'S MAGIC

Witchcraft began with magic, and was actually a step toward greater knowledge. Early magicians were something like scientists, trying to understand the forces of nature and so control them.

Cave paintings made by magicians, or sorcerers, of Europe twenty thousand years ago may still be seen today. Most are pictures of reindeer, mammoths, or other large animals lying trapped or pierced with spears.

The sorcerers believed that by painting a picture of something happening, they could make it happen. This is known as *imitative magic*.

To cast a spell on an enemy, the sorcerer would steal a piece of the person's clothing, a

20

lock of hair, or a bit of fingernail. When the enemy found out, he would be sick with fear and might even die. This was *contagious magic*.

Sometimes, to bewitch or kill, the sorcerer used *sympathetic magic*, burning or sticking pins into a tiny model of the person.

Sorcerers also had a knowledge of plant and animal products that seemed magical. They were experts at mixing medicines as well as poisons.

The sorcerer's knowledge of magic and medicine gave him a special power over the people around him. In order to retain this power, he kept his magic *occult*, or hidden.

When people began to farm, rain and sunshine became more important to them. Now they looked to the sorcerers to end dry spells and periods of cloudiness or of too much rain. But, as often as not, the sorcerer's magic failed.

Helpless before the forces of nature, people made them into gods. A human being could appeal to the nature gods, honor, flatter, or even threaten them, but never control them.

21

Whatever happened was the will of the gods. To interpret it, priests came into being.

Magicians and witches dropped into the background. Living at the fringes of ancient societies, they told fortunes, prepared charms and brewed herb mixtures for various ailments. In Rome and Greece they were considered harmless until A.D. 14, when Emperor Augustus Caesar banned them for fear their predictions might aid his rivals. In Israel, witches and magicians were banished, but some lived on there, undercover.

According to the Bible, King Saul himself secretly visited the Witch of Endor when he was worried about a coming battle. The witch called up Samuel from the dead to ask about Saul's future.

Angry at being summoned by a forbidden art, Samuel predicted that Saul would lose the battle and lose his life. And so he did.

By the time Christianity became the official Roman religion, using magic to blight a crop, raise a storm, or predict the death of an emperor was a serious crime. However, harmless magic—healing the sick or preparing love potions—was accepted.

Most magicians and witches were pagans. So, as the Christian church grew, they passed from favor, less for their magic than for their religious beliefs.

Many people, though, especially those in remote places in Europe, still held fast to their old beliefs—including their belief in magic, witches, and witchcraft.

THE HORNED GOD

In the seventh century, the Archbishop of Canterbury, England, set punishments for "those who goeth about in the masque of a stag or a bull-calf . . . those who by their craft raise storms . . . sacrifice to demons . . . consulteth soothsayers who divine by birds."

The people described by the Archbishop worshiped a horned god. Usually this was a bull, ram, or goat, but sometimes a man or woman wearing skins and the head of an animal.

In their magical rites, these people danced about in a circle, barking and howling. At midnight, using a bronze sickle, they gathered herbs. They cast spells or bewitched an enemy by sticking thorns into a wax model of the person. They brewed love potions and concocted poisons.

Into their cauldrons went the skins of snakes and the saliva and intestines of animals. At the end of the ceremony they sacrificed and ate the animal god. Their rites and ceremonies expressed their closeness to all animal life, and their desire to help it increase.

24

These worshipers were members of a religion handed down from the Stone Age, perhaps by the Little People. Life in the Stone Age had depended on the hunting and, later, on the raising of animals. Animal life was, therefore, sacred and godlike.

Even though the Christian religion was spreading, the religion of the horned god lingered on. In the tenth century, King Edgar of England admitted that it was more popular than Christianity. Its followers came to be known as witches.

At weekly meetings called *esbats* the witches of a village would gather in a home or in the open for instruction in magic.

25

Magical rites and ceremonies were performed by the *coven*, a band of men and women from a district under the rule of a grand master. In England, covens were made up of thirteen people, twelve witches and the master.

Several times a year, at Witches' Sabbaths, groups of witches from all over a region or country gathered at a sacred spot. The Blocula in Sweden was one such place, the Puy-de-Dôme in France another. The most famous sacred spot for witches was in the Hartz mountain region of Germany. Until the eighteenth century, maps of Germany showed witches hovering over this spot.

One of the most important Witches' Sabbaths came on the eve of May Day, a date sacred to the mating of animals. The other, at Halloween, recalled the date of early hunting ceremonies, when magicians or medicine men had acted out the capture of animals.

The Sabbaths were joyful, and people looked forward to them. Sometimes thousands attended. Among them were members of noble or royal families, their faces concealed by masks.

The assembled witches vowed to obey their god, the master disguised as an animal. They kissed him on whatever part of his body he chose, and paid homage by turning *widder-shins*—from west to east—a certain number of times. They pledged their children to the god and thanked him as the source of food and of life itself.

New witches were initiated, and witch couples were married. Then came the religious ceremonies, followed by feasting and dancing.

At spring Sabbaths there were jumping dances. The higher the witches jumped, the higher the crops would grow. Or so they believed.

At Halloween Sabbaths witches did dances to make animals more fertile, dressing up like animals themselves. To encourage fertility in human beings, they danced naked or in their usual clothes. In some of the dances they galloped about straddling branches or broomsticks.

As they danced, the witches chanted. Before long, the rhythmic movements, the rhythmic sounds, and the feeling of being at one with their horned god gave them a sense of ecstasy.

28

Some witches had been born into the religion. Others, including many learned men, were attracted by the magic practices. Still others joined in resentment against the Christian church. To a downtrodden peasant, the excitement of the witch cult had more appeal than the droning services held at church.

Many who joined were women. Few members of their sex had any status then. All were looked on as men's inferiors. Almost all were little more than their husbands' property. In the witch cult, they found equality.

For most people of the time—overworked and underfed—life was bleak. So they reached toward anything, like the witch cult, that promised release and joy.

A WAR ON THE DEVIL

In the Hebrew and Christian religions there had been devils and demons. The Devil with a capital *D* is a late Christian idea and refers to the New Testament Satan.

In Christian tradition, Satan was created good, but chose to become evil. Rebelling against God, he was cast out of heaven and became the tempter of humanity and the source of all evil.

By the Middle Ages the Devil had taken on the appearance of a suave, evil-looking man with horns, a forked tail, and cloven hooves. The prince of all demons and devils, he was described as powerful enough to destroy the established church.

Besides the members of witch cults, there were, at the time, individuals and groups who held different religious views from those of the Christian church. What if they grew in numbers and became rivals? To churchmen, the prospect was alarming.

So the church branded all such people as evil and emissaries of the Devil, the archenemy of the church. In the name of a war on the Devil, churchmen began a campaign against the *heretics*, as these people were called.

In the thirteenth century, Courts of Inquisition were set up, and thousands of people were tried. The judges sometimes accused people of witchcraft, but to sentence them the judges had to find them guilty of heresy. Witchcraft was mentioned at the trial of Joan of Arc, who led the French armies to victory over the English in 1429. But Joan was burned as a heretic and not as a witch.

Then, in 1484, Pope Innocent VIII issued a paper attacking witches as the Devil's agents. Soon people were being tried for witchcraft alone.

THE GREAT WITCH-HUNTS

Father James Sprenger and Father Henry Kramer, chief inquisitors for Germany, wrote a book called *The Hammer of Witches*. Witches were everywhere, the book warned. It told how to find witches, how to trick them into confessing, and how to torture and exterminate them.

Judges traveled from town to town, urging people to name suspects. Neighbor turned on neighbor. If a farmer's cow went dry, he might accuse some poor old woman of having bewitched it.

Anyone, even the smallest child, could testify, and children sometimes accused their own parents. Kings and queens named relatives who were trying to oust them from their thrones.

There were three degrees of witchcraft.

One was *white magic,* the use of charms and spells in harmless ways. A farmwife might mutter spells to speed up her buttermaking, for instance. The punishment for such white magic was seldom more than a rebuke from the neighborhood priest or minister.

33

Black Magic was more serious—working with the Devil to cause sickness or death, to raise storms, or to blight crops.

The most serious degree of all was signing *a pact with the Devil.* Judges delighted in showing such pacts in court. Few have survived, and those that have are probably fakes.

The most famous pact bears the signature of Urbain Grandier. A French priest, he was accused of bewitching all the nuns of a certain convent. There are weird symbols at the bottom of the contract. These were said to be the names of a whole committee of devils.

At a witchcraft trial, the suspect's body was searched for Devil's marks, supposedly placed there at the time of his initiation into the cult. Any birthmark, mole, wart, corn, or pimple would do.

English witches were often accused of having a "familiar" spirit or imp, disguised as a small animal, to help carry out the work of the Devil. They were also questioned in detail about the Witches' Sabbaths to which they were said to fly on broomsticks.

No witch could be put to death without confessing. Under torture, though, many who were not witches at all confessed, and real witches often confessed to deeds they had never done.

The courts worked overtime. The prisons filled. People awaiting trial might lie in their cells for years. Even if proved innocent, they were not released until someone had paid for their keep.

For some men, witch-hunting became a career. In England, in the 1600s, Matthew Hopkins set himself up as Witchfinder General. With two assistants, he traveled from place to place. One of his proudest possessions was a notebook filled with the names of witches. Where did he get it? He had tricked the Devil into giving it to him—or so he said.

With a special pin, he would go over the prisoner's body to find the Devil's mark, a

35

spot that felt no pain. After the mark was found, a guard waited for the prisoner's imp to arrive. This might be nothing more than an ant or a spider.

In Hopkins' swimming test, suspects were placed in water. Those who floated were declared guilty of witchcraft and quickly sentenced. Those who sank fared no better, for the onlookers cried out for further tests.

After three years of such cruelty, no one felt safe. Then a country minister began preaching against Hopkins, who was barred from the next town. Before long, Hopkins was seized himself. Given the water test and failing to sink, he was sent to the gallows.

The witch-hunt went on in Europe for nearly three hundred years, reaching its peak in the seventeenth century. How many people were burned or hanged, no one is sure. Some say nine million.

During this time, the Protestant Reformation had begun in a spirit of questioning the established church. In regard to witches, however, the Protestants were even more violent than the Catholics. To justify it, they quoted such passages from the Bible as "Thou shalt not suffer a witch to live."

Across the Atlantic in the Plymouth Colony, the penalty for witchcraft was death, but no one was ever executed. There was one witch-hanging in Boston in 1648 and another in Connecticut a few years later. Then, in 1692, two children of Salem Village, now Danvers, Massachusetts, set off a witch-hunt that sent twenty people to their deaths.

From Salem, the witch scare quickly spread to other towns, until no one felt safe. Within a year or so, the madness died down.

The worst was over, but American witch-hunting had not ended. As late as 1730, Benjamin Franklin reported a witch trial in the pages of the *Pennsylvania Gazette*.

Scholars who see the witch cult as the survival of an ancient Stone Age religion feel that it really could have become a rival of the Christian church. This, they believe, was the true reason for all the witch-hunts.

THE WITCH ENTERS HALLOWEEN

By the nineteenth century, few educated people anywhere took witchcraft very seriously. An English dictionary called it "a pretended magic or sorcery in which our ancestors believed."

People with less education, though, especially those far from cities, went right on believing in witches. The goblins and other beings they had always feared at Halloween were now thought of mainly as witches.

To scare them away, Scottish farmers carried blazing torches from west to east across their fields. Farmers of the Pennsylvania Dutch country printed hex signs on their barns to ward off witches all the year.

Witches and fairies, it was said, refused to touch either iron or salt. So many country people put some of each by the bed of a new-born child.

According to another saying, the shell of a boiled egg should be cracked at the bottom. Otherwise a witch might use the shell as a boat.

All of these precautions were most important at Halloween, when witches were said to be flying about.

WITCHES TODAY

Reminders are all around us today of a time when people believed in witches. Barns in the Pennsylvania Dutch country still have hex signs—added, the owners say, for decoration. In country districts of Europe and the United States, there are still "wise women," who mix herb potions and tell fortunes. In the larger cities, little shops sell charms and love potions.

In England and the United States, in recent years, people calling themselves witches have come into the open. Among them are students, housewives, businessmen and women, and others.

Some claim to be Satanists, who worship the Devil. Many say they are reviving the Stone Age fertility religion. Others see in magic and the occult a "higher wisdom." They cast horoscopes by means of the stars or read magical meanings from the number of letters in a person's name.

JIM
194
5

THE STORYBOOK WITCH

Meanwhile, in legends, stories, poems, and pictures an image of the witch as we know her took shape.

The real witches of olden times had included men as well as women, children and young people as well as the old. This was forgotten. The storybook witch is usually a women, usually evil, and usually old.

41

As such, she takes the leading role at Halloween today. A symbol of the evil spirits once thought to emerge at this time of year, she is an ugly old woman, with matted hair, bony fingers, a broomstick, and cat.

If not scanned too closely, the Halloween witch is just colorful and part of the holiday fun. Actually, she is a distortion of history and perhaps a disservice to women in their struggle for equality.

The Witch's Familiars

On Halloween cards, in party decorations, and in Halloween stories, the witch almost always appears with at least a cat. Sometimes she is shown not only with a cat but with owls, bats, and toads, as well. These are the witch's *familiars*. In the Middle Ages, many witches admitted to having one or more.

A *divining familiar* was the species of animal whose shape the "Devil" would take to help the witch in divining the future. A witch trying to find out the length of a person's life or of an illness would watch the familiar closely. The speed or slowness of the animal's movements, the direction in which it moved, the kinds of sounds it made—all these were considered clues.

The *domestic familiar,* or imp, might be a hen or goose, a cat, a small dog, a rat, an owl or toad—even a butterfly or a wasp. The imp was kept in a box or an earthen pot. Fed on bread and milk mixed with drops of blood, it was said to assist the witch with her magic.

43

A witch might have one imp or several. In 1645, Mother Lakeland, of Ipswich, England, confessed that the Devil had given her two little dogs and a mole.

Anne Cate, brought to trial at Chelmsford by Witchfinder General Matthew Hopkins, admitted to having four familiars. Three were mice named James, Prickeare, and Robyn. The fourth was a sparrow. Anne confessed that she dispatched them to kill cattle and human beings.

A witch's familiar was considered her double. If the imp was wounded, the witch would suffer. If the imp died, the witch would die.

But killing imps was very difficult. A man in Chelmsford passed the house of Anne West one moonlight night, when "three or four little things in the shape of black rabbits" came leaping at him. Convinced that they were imps, he tried to beat them to death. Then, catching hold of one, he tried to wring its neck. Next, he tried to take it to a spring, but kept stumbling and falling down. Finally, creeping to the water on hands and knees, he held the creature under water for a long time. As soon as he let go, it sprang out of the water and vanished.

A farmer whose wife was having trouble with her buttermaking was more successful. In this case the suspect was a blue butterfly. For three weeks it had hovered over the farm. And for three weeks the farmwife had churned her cream without getting any butter.

Determined to break the spell, the farmer chased the butterfly with a towel and brought it down. At the moment the butterfly died, a woman in the neighborhood was found dead at her home.

After that there was no further trouble with the churning. Of course not, the farmer and his wife decided. The blue butterfly had been this same woman in disguise. When they boasted to their neighbors of having rid the world of a troublesome witch, no one questioned it.

In London, a rooster said to be a witch's familiar was once summoned to court and tried by a group of learned judges. And no one saw anything ridiculous in this.

The Halloween Cat

In a classroom where children are asked to draw Halloween pictures of their own choosing, almost everyone draws a witch, a Jack-O'-Lantern, or a black cat—the most popular symbols of the holiday.

Long before there was a Halloween, cats were thought to have magical powers. They were first tamed in ancient Egypt to keep the grain storehouses free of rats and mice. The Egyptians worshiped a cat-headed goddess named Pasht. They carved cat statues and designed furniture and jewelry in the shape of cats.

Hecate, a goddess of the ancient Greeks and Romans, ruled over witches, wizards, and ghosts. Hecate's priestess was a cat that had once been a woman.

The Phoenicians, who lived at the eastern end of the Mediterranean Sea in ancient times, carried cats with them aboard their ships. In western Europe, they traded the cats for precious tin.

The cat was one of the animals sacred to Freya, Norse goddess of beauty, love, and marriage—and of the dead. According to Norse myth, at the end of a battle Freya was entitled to one-half of the warriors slain. She was said to come for them in a chariot drawn by cats.

Among the Druids, cats were dreaded as human beings changed into animals by evil powers. At the festival on November 1, a number of cats were always thrown into the Samhain fires.

But why should the Halloween cat be black? A cat serving as a witch's familiar could be any color. Among five witches accused of tormenting a certain English family was Elizabeth Dickenson, whose familiar was a white cat. Thomas Rabbet, aged eight, reported that his mother kept several "spirites," one of them "like a little grey Cat."

Black, white, gray, yellow, striped, or calico, a cat found guilty of being a witch's familiar was killed with the witch.

Long after the witch-hunts, people went on accusing one another of witchcraft. They believed that witches not only had cats as familiars but could change into cats themselves.

47

After dark, with everything dim and shadowy, all cats looked black. And so, as time went on, a witch's cat was thought of as being black.

Never knowing whether a cat was an innocent pet or a witch in disguise, people suspected them all, especially at Halloween.

They pointed out how stealthy cats were, moving noiselessly about on their padded paws. They distrusted the sinister glare of their yellow eyes, and the fact that cats could see well at night while they could not.

There were sayings like these:

Honest as a cat when the cream is out of reach.

Never let a cat into the same room with a corpse. It might be a demon and turn the dead soul into a vampire.

A cat that sits with its back to the fire is raising a storm.

A ship with a cat on board is never wrecked, for the cat acts as a counter-charm.

A cat's behavior at Halloween, when visits from spirits were expected, sent tingles of fear along people's spines. A curtain might flutter or a timber creak. There might be a mournful wailing in the wind. At these signs of the spirits, the family dog would bristle and slink away. The cat sat unperturbed.

No wonder, people said, the cat was probably a spirit itself.

Along with the fear of cats went attempts to benefit by their magic. If a cat rubs against you, expect good luck, a saying went. If it yawns, opportunity awaits.

Young girls served boys they liked love potions made of tea and dried cat's liver. Irish people declared that a charm made of the bone of a black cat could make one invisible.

Linked with the Druid Samhain and, later, with witches, the cat found a permanent place in Halloween. Its back arched, its hair on end, its yellow eyes glaring, the cat stood for the spirit of evil.

The Owl—Harbinger of Evil

In Edward Lear's famous poem, the owl and the pussycat set off to sea on a merry and innocent voyage. At Halloween, owls and cats travel with witches.

In ancient Rome owls were considered harbingers of evil, while in Greece they were sacred. The owl was a familiar of Athene, Greek goddess of wisdom. This may be why owls are thought of as being wise.

Europeans of the Middle Ages feared the glassy stare and eerie call of the owl, as the Romans had. The screech owl in particular made them think of witches.

50

Screech owls nested in hollow trees, seldom giving a sign of their presence until nightfall. Their weird, trembling call and hollow whistle frightened travelers on lonely roads. It sounded so witchlike. It might actually *be* a witch, hiding among the trees. For witches, as everyone agreed, often took other shapes.

In Grimms' tale of *Jorinda and Joringel,* an owl circles overhead, screeching, when the girl and boy venture too close to a witch's castle. The boy, Joringel, is struck motionless and speechless. Jorinda turns into a nightingale. The owl disappears into a thicket, and a bent old woman comes out. When she takes the nightingale away in a basket, Joringel realizes that she is a witch.

Even today, superstitious people in some places believe the sound of the screech owl means death or disaster.

Along with cats, bats, and witches, the owl continues to stare at us in late October from greeting cards and party decorations, adding its bit to the eeriness of Halloween.

The Mysterious Bat

A creature of the night, seldom seen at close range, and the only mammal that flies, the bat found its way into Halloween long ago.

Early pictures of witches show them worshiping a horned figure that sometimes had the wings of a bat. Bat blood was an ingredient in the ointment that witches rubbed on their bodies before attending a Sabbath. The wings and entrails of bats went into their brews.

When the Christian church of the Middle Ages waged its war on pagan religions, any creature related to them came under suspicion. Bats, like cats, had been sacred to the Norse goddess Freya. Now they were linked with witches—another "proof" that they were evil.

Bats were frightening in themselves. Their heads had such weird shapes. Some were like the heads of tiny bulldogs. Others looked like miniature bears, with long, menacing, pointed teeth.

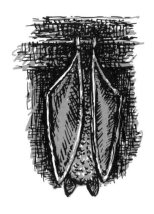

And what enormous wings they had! With a body only two inches long, a bat might have a wingspread of one foot.

Bats could fly about on the darkest night, guided, it seemed, by some mysterious, evil power. How else did they find their way?

They took cover in dark caverns or the depths of a forest, in empty barns or abandoned houses. By day, they hung upside down from branch, roof, or ceiling, their wings draped around them like witches' cloaks.

A few kinds of tropical bats are dangerous. One is the vampire bat, which lives on the blood of other animals, including human beings. Most bats are useful, though. They eat vast numbers of harmful insects.

Flying through the night, bats emit high-pitched sounds that strike objects in the path of their flight. Echoes, bouncing back, enable the bats to avoid collisions.

Modern scientists call this radar. In the days of the witch-hunts, however, little scientific knowledge of animals existed. And what people could not understand, they naturally feared.

53

The Unpopular Toad

At the time of the witch scare, most
people in Europe lived on farms or in
small villages. There were toads in their gardens, under their porches, in the fields, and
along the roadside. In wet weather or at dawn
or dusk, the toads crept out to stalk cutworms,
moths, and snails.

54

Rocks were thrown at toads, for they were considered poisonous. When a dog chased a toad, people had noticed, the dog might come away with a sore mouth or sore eyes. If they handled a toad themselves, their own eyes or nose might burn or itch.

No wonder, people said, that so many witches made familiars of toads. Mother Dutton of Windsor freely admitted it. At her trial, she described the spirit or fiend in the likeness of a toad that she kept in her herb garden, feeding it with drops of her blood.

Other witches told of mixing the spittle of a toad or bits of its body into their brews. A toad boiled in the bubbling cauldron of the three Weird Sisters in William Shakespeare's play *Macbeth* . . .

> Round about the caldron go;
> In the poisoned entrails throw.
> Toad, that under the cold stone,
> Days and nights hast thirty-one
> Swelter'd venom sleeping got,
> Boil thou first i' the charmed pot!

A toad does not spit out poison, as was once thought. To protect itself, when in danger, it gives off a certain substance. This substance can irritate the eyes, nose, or mouth of a dog or a human being.

A toad absorbs water through its skin, and so really can change from small to large, or from large to small.

Instead of being man's enemy, the toad is a friend, eating cutworms and other creatures that damage plants.

A toad can be tamed and fed on bread and water. Unlike most pets, it has a long life-span, sometimes as much as thirty-five years.

Today it is considered unusual but harmless to tame a toad. But like the bat, the toad is still rather unpopular. With its warty skin, it is sometimes even blamed for causing warts in people. Appearing with witches in so many stories, the toad has become a small but continuing part of Halloween.

The Witch's Broomstick

Artists of the Middle Ages often showed witches preparing to fly off to one of their Sabbaths. They were usually rubbing themselves with something or being rubbed by someone else. This was the flying ointment.

Angels and devils were supposed to be able to fly, so it was easy to believe that witches, too, could fly. Many witches believed it themselves. Before setting out for a Sabbath, they rubbed a sacred ointment into their pores. This gave them a feeling of flying. If they had been fasting, the ointment made them even giddier.

Those who were well-off rode on horseback. Poor witches went on foot. With them they carried a broom or pole for vaulting over brooks, streams, or thorny patches.

In England, when new witches were initiated they were sometimes blindfolded, smeared with flying ointment, and placed astride a broom. One substance in the ointment confused the mind. Another speeded up the witch's pulse. Still another numbed the feet.

When the master whispered, "You are flying over land and sea," the new witch took his word for it.

The other witches then began a chant:

Horse and hattock,
Horse and go,
Horse and pellatis
Ho, Ho!

No wonder that the Halloween witch is often pictured riding or holding a broomstick.

Fire Burn and Cauldron Bubble

Sometimes the Halloween witch is shown stirring a brew in a large cooking pot.

Witches of old, setting out for a Sabbath, often had long distances to go. They were seen on country roads, alone or in chattering groups, laden down with bundles of food and large cooking cauldrons.

At the meeting place the witches gathered firewood, fresh herbs, and ripe berries, and looked for water. Then, with three stout green branches they fashioned a tripod to hold the cauldron.

Soon a broth flavored with herbs and berries was bubbling above a crackling fire. Horseflesh, sacred to pagan gods, was roasted in the coals.

Travelers coming upon a scene like this at night were frightened. They told afterwards of seeing the witches peer into their cauldrons,

cackling and smacking their lips, the firelight giving their weird faces an eerie glow.

> Fillet of a fenny snake,
> In the caldron boil and bake;
> Eye of newt, and toe of frog,
> Wool of bat, and tongue of dog,
> Adder's fork, and blind-worm's sting,
> Lizard's leg, and howlet's wing,
> For a charm of powerful trouble,
> Like a hell-broth boil and bubble.

This is the recipe of the Second Weird Sister in Shakespeare's *Macbeth*. Audiences in London theaters in Shakespeare's time saw nothing surprising about the witch's brew. People who practiced witchcraft really did concoct such mixtures for casting spells.

Most women of the time brewed cauldrons of herbs to cure headaches and backaches, fevers and colds. But a lonely old woman, who was not a witch, might be overheard talking to herself as she stirred her brew. Before long she might find herself accused of causing measles in a neighbor's children or of blinding a neighbor's horse.

60

Halloween Ghosts

After dark on Halloween, flitting from house to house, there are always at least a few figures draped in sheets, white and ghostly against the night.

At Halloween parties, it is fun to listen to frightening but thrilling stories. With the lights out and with wails and moans coming from a closet, the effect is more chilling still. Since we know the ghost in the closet won't harm us, we only pretend to be afraid.

There was nothing make-believe about the fears of the Scotch, Irish, and English on this same evening years ago. This was the night when ghosts, the spirits or disembodied souls of the dead, were thought to return to their former homes, looking for warmth and cheer. To displease the ghosts was dangerous, for they could punish you.

By now the harvest was in. The cattle had returned from their summer pastures to be fed and sheltered in winter stalls. A farmer and his wife could hardly deny the ghosts of relatives the same welcome they gave their cows. So, on Samhain Eve, a fire was kept burning, and the table was heaped with food. Otherwise, angry or envious ghosts might steal the newly harvested food, destroy animals, or kidnap children.

A waving branch, a stir in the bushes, a winged shape darting suddenly from a tree— on Samhain Eve anything like this was considered the sign of a ghost. People tried to keep away from lonely places.

Indoors, they heard the wild winds of autumn howling, wailing, or shrieking. "*Ghosts!*" they would tell one another in trembling voices.

Throughout Gaul and Britain, huge Samhain fires lighted the skies above hilltops. Their bright flames were meant to guide kindly ghosts on their journeys home and frighten evil ones away. For ghosts were not thought of as all good or all bad. Like the living, they were a mixture. There was no way of knowing which side they would show—good or bad.

Hundreds of years after All Hallows' Eve had replaced Samhain, people still built up their fires and piled their tables with tempting food. Then, leaving the door unlocked, they went to church.

Usually when they came back, the food was gone. If it remained, they thought that they had displeased their relatives' ghosts. When beggars and tramps began taking not only the food but silverware and valuables as well, the custom died out.

Cut off from the rest of France, the people of Brittany clung to pagan beliefs long after others had given them up—especially to the cult of death. All around them were reminders of the Druids: ancient stone altars and *dolmens*, the tombs made of one enormous flat rock resting like a roof on two others.

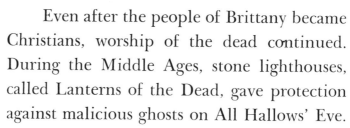

Even after the people of Brittany became Christians, worship of the dead continued. During the Middle Ages, stone lighthouses, called Lanterns of the Dead, gave protection against malicious ghosts on All Hallows' Eve.

Until fairly recent times in Brittany, a bellman went around before midnight on the eve of All Souls' Day to warn that the ghosts were coming.

In each home a supper for the souls was set out. And after everyone was in bed, death singers made their rounds:

You are comfortably lying in your bed,
But with the poor dead it is otherwise:
You are stretched softly in your bed
While the poor souls are wandering abroad.
ANATOLE LE BRAZ, *Night of the Dead*

People used to think it could be very dangerous, even fatal, to meet a ghost face-to-face on Halloween. But they feared them throughout the year. When even the driest

64

wood refused to burn, they blamed a ghost for chilling the air.

Rings were left on the fingers of sick people to keep ghosts or demons from entering the body. To free the spirit of a dead person, rings were removed.

Children born on Halloween were said to be able to see ghosts and even talk with them. On this night when so many ghosts were abroad, they might reveal themselves to ordinary people, too, and give warnings or advice.

Halloween became the night of all nights for divining the future. Older people tried to find out how long they would live. Young people were more interested in whom they would marry.

A Halloween custom of Scotch and Irish girls was called *the wetting of the sark sleeve.* It had once been a rite in honor of Freya, the Norse goddess of love and marriage.

The girl would wash a fine piece of linen in a running stream. One hour before midnight, she hung it up to dry before the fire.

At half-past eleven, she had to turn it. At twelve, the spirit of her future husband was supposed to appear. Often, a girl fell asleep waiting, dreamed of the man she loved, and thought she had seen his spirit.

Every town or village had at least one old deserted house that was said to be haunted. People reported hearing creaks and tapping, the sound of footsteps, or a wailing they felt sure was more than the wind. Everyone dreaded passing one of these haunted houses at night, especially on Halloween.

Some neighborhoods had ghost animals. The churchyard might be haunted by a large white rabbit or a hound as big as a calf, with one enormous red eye. To meet one of these creatures or to hear it howling was a warning of death.

People of all religions have special days dedicated to the dead.

The Tuaregs, a wandering people of the Sahara, visit graves on the first day of the Mohammedan month of *Ramadan*. People of the Jewish faith usually do this in the month of *Tishri*.

66

On the island of Bali, near Indonesia, an-cestral spirits are believed to return during the first five weeks of the Buddhist year.

The Hopi Indians summon the dead to a festival at the summer solstice, when the sun is highest in the heavens.

In Naples, Italy, relatives of the dead pen-cil their names on the tombs and leave calling cards on All Souls' Day.

On the same day, in French churches the bright flowers and glowing candles give way to black drapings, funeral songs, and prayers for the dead.

In Latin America, Halloween as we cele-brate it is unknown, but, for centuries, this was a night of ghosts. Men and boys went from house to house, singing *alabanzas* to the spirits of the dead. They avoided lonely roads and were careful to stay together.

Families with children who had died set out cakes, candies, and toys for the child angels. Some parents set off firecrackers to guide their *angelito* homeward.

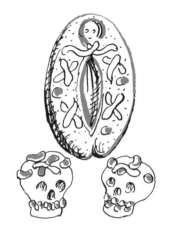

Today the former customs and rites for the Days of the Dead have vanished in most of Latin America. In a few isolated parts of Mexico they remain—in Puebla, for example, and in Oaxaca, where the Zapotec Indians still hold to ancestral ways.

There the Days of the Dead, November 1 and 2, are a joyous fiesta, for the Indians accept death and can even joke about it. Children look forward to the holiday and enjoy eating the Bread of the Dead. These are little loaves sprinkled with colored sugar, sometimes shaped like people. Each represents a dead soul.

In the United States, Memorial Day in May was first established to honor soldiers who had died in battle. Now it has widened to include all the dead. People tidy up the family graves and decorate them with fresh flowers.

American Halloween ghosts may seem to have little to do with the spirits of our ancestors. But they came here with people who did think of them in that way—the Scotch and the Irish, ancestors of many Americans.

Rattling Bones

"I'm a shade of my former self," said
    the skeleton.
"I shiver and shake like so much gela-
    tine,
Indeed I'm a pitiful sight to see—
I'm scareder of *kids* than they are of
    me!"

MARGARET FISHBACK

In a spooky Halloween story, in costumes
and decorations, or on Halloween greeting
cards, skeletons mean the same thing as Halloween ghosts. They remind us once again
that a holiday we celebrate just for fun was
once solemn—a day of the dead.

The skulls and skeletons of Halloween
are horrible in a pleasant, spine-tingling way.
Real skulls and skeletons make us think of
death.

A few centuries ago, with no modern
medicines or surgery, people lived shorter
lives, but their religion consoled them with
the promise of a life to come. A skull with
crossbones was less disturbing then than it is

70

today. Those on early New England tombstones often look remarkably cheerful.

In many countries today, people have this same attitude toward human remains.

"We live with our dead," the French people of Brittany say. On the eve of All Souls, they go to the cemetery to pray for departed souls. At the "place of bones," the remains of those dead for a long time lie together in one tomb. People press up to iron gratings to peer at the bones. At the entrance to the tomb, they walk along, touching the rows of skulls. Doing this makes them feel closer to their ancestors.

The eve of All Souls in Naples, Italy, finds everyone at the cemeteries, dressing up the exposed skeletons of dead relatives. On All Souls' Day itself, the skeletons receive visitors in their tombs.

In Mexico on the Days of the Dead, street peddlers sell holiday toys. There are skeletons with movable legs and toy coffins that release a skeleton Jack-in-the-box. The special jewelry on sale includes tiepins in the shape of a skeleton with dangling ribs.

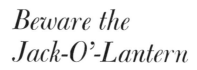

Beware the Jack-O'-Lantern

In 1900 an English lady asked the horseman on her country estate if he had ever noticed any ghosts.

"Ghosties!" he scoffed. "Who's believing in them? All I've ever seen about the place is Lantern Men. I've seen them running around scores of times."

Some people called the Lantern Men Hob-O'-Lantern, Jack-O'-Lantern, Will-O'-the-Wisp, or Will. A pale eerie light that appeared over bogs and marshes bobbed along like a lantern in someone's hand.

The sight sometimes made a farmer's horse shy and tip his cart into the ditch. A person on foot would run for his very life.

One farmer in Kent told of being followed home by a Jack-O'-Lantern. There, shivering and shaking, the farmer jumped into bed and pulled the covers over his head. When he finally got up enough courage to look out, the Jack-O'-Lantern was at his window.

The first thing to do if you met one was to put out your own lantern. Otherwise, Jack would come up and dash it to pieces. If he came this close, you should throw yourself on the ground and hold your breath. Advice like this was passed around from person-to-person.

The ghostly lights that hovered over graves dug in marshy places were called Corpse Candles. Fishermen in Kent used to see them above a treacherous swampland on the coast. They believed them to be signals from souls of men lost at sea. They said it meant that the men wanted to be buried when their bodies washed ashore. If even a bone or two could be found, the ghost would be laid to rest and the Corpse Candles put out.

In places where the strange lights were known as Will-O'-the-Wisp, people warned one another never to follow one. The Will-O'-the-Wisp would lead a person to a watery death in the deepest, most dangerous part of the swamp.

What was the strange flickering light that so many people said they had met or seen?

Scientists call it *ignis fatuus*, meaning foolish fire. It may be something like the phos-

phorescense that gives the firefly its flashing light. Or it may come from the spontaneous combustion of methane, the marsh gas that burns so easily. The gas is given off by rotting plant and animal forms in places with little oxygen. The same gas is found in the *firedamp* that causes mine explosions.

Before this was known, some people imagined that Jack-O'-Lanterns were the souls of sinners condemned to walk the earth till the end of time.

An Irish story tells of a ne'er-do-well named Stingy Jack, who, one Halloween, invited the Devil to have a drink.

"If you pay for it," the Devil replied.

"But you can change into any shape you choose," Jack protested. "Change yourself in-

to a sixpence. After I've paid for the drink, you can change yourself back."

The Devil agreed. He muttered a spell, disappeared, and there on the counter was a shiny new sixpence.

But Stingy Jack popped the coin into his pocket, where a silver cross prevented the Devil from getting out. "If you'll let me alone for a year, I'll let you out, "Jack said.

The Devil promised, and was released. Jack intended to reform. He meant to take his pay home to his wife, to go to church, and give to the poor. But as soon as he was out of danger, he went back to his former ways.

The following Halloween he met the Devil on a lonely road. "He's come for my soul!" thought Jack. This time he tricked the Devil into sparing him for ten years. But before a year had passed, Jack died. Turned back

at the gates of heaven, he made his way to the gates of hell.

"Go away," the Devil shouted. "Go back where you came from. You tricked me, and made me promise not to claim your soul.

"But it's dark," said Jack. "How can I find my way?"

The Devil threw him a glowing coal. Jack put it inside a turnip. And ever since, with this Jack-O'-Lantern, he has been roaming the face of the earth.

At Halloween, Scottish children look for the largest turnips from the harvest. They hollow them out, carve faces on them, and put candles inside. They call them bogies and carry them to scare away witches.

Irish children use turnips or potatoes. In parts of England, children carry "punkies."

Made of large beets known as *mangel-wurzels*, they are hollowed out and have a window through which the candle shines.

When Scotch and Irish people came to the United States, they found pumpkins growing here. With their brilliant color, their round shapes and soft insides, pumpkins made perfect Jack-O'-Lanterns, as they do still.

In Sycamore, Illinois, about a week before Halloween, "pumpkin fever" breaks out. Everyone gets ready for the pumpkin contest. In a few days, hundreds of decorated pumpkins will cover the courthouse lawn, and prizes will be awarded the best. There is a pumpkin pie-baking contest and a contest to see who can eat the most. At the end of the festival comes the pumpkin parade.

The festival really begins the spring before, when pumpkin seeds are passed out. The children plant their seeds and watch them grow all through the summer and fall.

Black and Orange

The black of a witch's cloak and the orange of a Jack-O'-Lantern remind us that Halloween was once a harvest festival as well as a festival of the dead.

Orange and deep yellow are the colors most common in ripened fruits, vegetables, and grains. In the language of colors, orange

78

is a symbol of strength and endurance. Together with brown, it stands for autumn and harvest. It is also the color of flames that once rose from dark hilltops on October 31 to ward off evil spirits.

Today, in most countries black is the color for death. From earliest times, people feared the night. Robbing them of the power to see clearly, it turned familiar objects into frightening shapes. In its blackness lurked the threat of death—from an evil spirit, another person, or a wild beast.

The Druids established the night of October 31 as a gathering time for the spirits of death and evil. The witches of the Middle Ages were thought of as evil beings who flew through the night to secret meetings, one of these on Halloween.

No wonder that the witch has come down to us, in stories and legends, cloaked in black, the color of death and night, her companion a black cat.

Nuts, Apples, and Cabbages Predict the Future

Halloween parties are filled with symbols of the harvest—cornstalks and pumpkins, apples and apple cider, nuts, popcorn, and candy corn. They remind us that the ancient Samhain festival that gave way to Halloween was not only a time of ghosts and spirits but also a joyous harvest festival.

Centuries after Samhain had merged into Halloween, people of Europe were still holding lively parties on October 31. Winter, with its cold, loneliness, and possible illness, lay ahead. Just now, at the harvest, food was plentiful, but who could say whether it would last until spring? For one evening, at least, people pushed all these fears aside.

Nuts and apples were not only a part of the feast. They were also used for telling fortunes on this magical night when charms, spells, and ways of finding out the future were believed to be most successful.

80

SNAP APPLE NIGHT

Apples had long been a token of love and fertility. Early Hebrew women who wanted children washed themselves in water mixed with the sap of an apple tree. The Norse gods were said to eat apples to keep them forever young.

At the first Halloween parties, people roasted and ate apples and bobbed for them in tubs of water. If a boy came up with a dripping apple between his teeth, it meant that he was loved by the girl he loved.

Boys also enjoyed the game of Snap Apple. Each boy in turn sprang up and tried to bite an apple that was twirled on the end of a stick. The first to succeed would be the first to marry. The game was so popular that Halloween was sometimes called Snap Apple Night.

Girls found out about their future husbands by paring apples, keeping the peeling in one long piece. This was swung three times around the head, then thrown over the left shoulder. A peeling that fell unbroken was supposed to form the initial of the girl's future husband.

81

Apple seeds were also used for telling fortunes. Seeds named for two different sweethearts were stuck on a girl's eyelids. The length of time the seeds stayed on showed which sweetheart was truer. Some girls helped the fates by winking one eye or twitching one cheek.

Placing twelve apple seeds on the palm of one hand and striking the palm with her other hand, a girl might repeat the following rhyme:

One I love,
Two I love,
Three I love, I say;
Four I love with all my heart;
Five I cast away.
Six he loves,
Seven she loves,
Eight they both love;
Nine he comes,
Ten he tarries,
Eleven he courts, and
Twelve he marries.

NUTCRACK NIGHT

In some parts of England, Scotland, and Ireland, nuts were so much a part of Halloween that the holiday was called Nutcrack Night. Long a symbol of life and fertility, the nuts that crackled and popped on the hearths were used to predict a person's love life.

Scottish young people put pairs of nuts named after certain couples before the fire. If a pair burned to ashes together, that couple would expect a happy life. If the nuts crackled or sprang apart, quarrels and separation could be expected.

On Irish hearths there were usually three nuts, named for one girl and two of her sweethearts. Whichever nut burned more steadily with the girl's told her which sweetheart would be more faithful.

In Wales, a brightly blazing nut meant prosperity. One that smouldered or popped foretold misfortune. There in Wales, where Druid customs had lasted so long, the nuts probably took the place of the animal sacrifices of earlier Samhain fires.

PULLING THE KALE

In Scotland, unengaged young people went out blindfolded to the vegetable garden. They each pulled up a stalk of kale, then trooped back to the house and removed their blindfolds.

A closed white stalk meant an elderly wife or husband, an open green one, a younger mate. To find out whether her future husband's disposition would be bitter or sweet, a girl tasted the stem. To find out his name, she hung the stalk with a row of others above the door. If Jenny's stalk hung third in line, and the third man to pass through the door was named Alan, Jenny believed that her future husband would bear that name.

In Ireland, cabbage stalks were named for different people at the Halloween party and then examined. A clean, light cabbage meant that the person it was named for would go to heaven. A cabbage darkened by frost meant that the person would go to hell.

Halloween Foods

No Irish Halloween was complete
without a huge serving of *caulcannon*,
a dish still eaten in Ireland today. Made of
mashed potatoes, parsnips, and onions, and
with tiny objects inside, it was another way of
telling fortunes. A coin in a portion of caulcannon meant wealth. A ring stood for marriage, a doll for children, a thimble for spin-
sterhood.

In the Hebrides Islands, off Scotland,
there were special Halloween cakes made of
meal and salt or salt herring. Anyone who went

to bed after eating it without drinking any water would expect to dream of receiving a drink from the future husband or wife.

In central and southern England, a special bread or cake was as important at Halloween as plum pudding at Christmas. The custom came from an old autumn tradition of baking bread from the new grain at the harvest festival.

Cakes were also served at the vigil of All Souls the following day. In return for a soul cake, each guest said prayers for the dead.

When English people first settled on American shores, there was little celebration of Halloween. But here and there, some of the English settlers continued the custom of apple-ducking and apple-snapping. And some of the girls tossed apple parings over their shoulders.

When the Scotch and Irish arrived, they held parties like the ones they had known at home. The refreshments and decorations showed the double meaning of Halloween— a festival of the natural and the supernatural. On the table there was usually a pumpkin

86

filled with nuts, apples, raisins, and other harvest fruits. Sometimes there was a pumpkin coach drawn by stuffed field mice. In the coach sat a tiny witch, a symbol of magic.

The young people bobbed for apples or snapped them from a whirling stick. As in the Old Country, the holiday was often known as Snap Apple Night or Nutcrack Night.

Marching to the table to the strains of a funeral dirge, the guests sat down to a feast of crisp doughnuts, golden gingerbread, pumpkin pie, cider, buttered popcorn, apples, and nuts.

Where cabbages grew, the girls pulled them up, hoping to see their future husbands at the party or on the way home.

Halloween was a country holiday. Then, more and more people left the land for jobs in the cities. With no gardens, they had to give up the custom of cabbage-pulling. But nuts, apples, cider, doughnuts, and pumpkin pie were still favorite Halloween refreshments, as they are today.

The Halloween Masquerade

A mask, even more than a costume, turns a person for the moment into someone else. At Halloween, horrible masks are a favorite part of the fun.

From earliest times, people all over the world have worn masks for more serious reasons. When droughts, epidemics, or other disasters struck, primitive people donned their most hideous masks. They hoped the demons that had brought the disaster would think they were demons, too, and be frightened off.

Among the witches of the Middle Ages,

88

it was not only the person representing the horned god who wore a mask. The witches often smeared their faces with soot and paint or put on masks. And people of the nobility attending a Witches' Sabbath always came masked.

Long after the festival of Samhain had merged with Halloween, people of Europe continued to feel uneasy at this time of year. Food was stored away against the winter; the house was snug and warm. But outside in the cold were envious ghosts, ready to strike. To keep from being recognized, people who went out after dark wore costumes and masks.

Until a few decades ago, boys and girls put on masks and dressed up as ghosts or witches to "scare" the neighbors, but no one went around trick-or-treating at Halloween.

Then, twenty or thirty years ago, people

began to offer candy or other treats to their costumed visitors. Soon children were knocking on doors and shouting "trick or treat!"

Each Halloween, more and more ghosts, witches, devils, goblins, pirates, Martians, and spacemen appeared with paper bags at people's doors. Then some children began to carry little boxes instead of bags, collecting money for the United Nations Children's Fund.

Although the purpose was different, this custom was far from new. In parts of England, the poor once went from house to house, singing and begging for soul cakes or money on the eve of All Saints.

Spanish people used to put cakes and nuts on graves after dark on Halloween. The gifts were bribes to keep evil spirits away.

Belgian children once stood beside little shrines in front of their homes, begging for money to buy cakes. They were taught that for each cake they ate, the suffering of one dead soul would be eased.

In Ireland, until the present century, masked figures went begging from farm to farm, in the name of Muck Olla, a Druid god. The verses they recited described the damage Muck Olla would do to a farmer's house or barn if the farmer refused to give something.

At the end of the evening, the masqueraders went home, loaded down with butter, eggs, cheese, corn, and potatoes.

91

Twenty-four hours after Halloween, on the eve of All Souls' Day, children of eastern Wales still go from house to house begging for soul cakes or for:

An apple or a pear, a plum, or a cherry,
Or any good thing to make us merry.

On October 31, French children beg for flowers to take to the cemeteries. They want to be ready for All Saints, the day that follows.

In areas where English children make mangel-wurzels into Jack-O'-Lanterns, they carry them from door to door. Singing songs, they receive coins or new candles.

Most holidays have both a serious and a lighter side. In the United States on the Fourth of July, firecrackers explode and people enjoy picnics in celebration of the nation's independence. Christmas, so full of gaiety, has, for many people, an important religious meaning. Halloween, with more ancient beginnings than any other holiday, no longer has any serious meaning. Children have kept it alive because they love it.

92

Dressed as ghosts, witches, skeletons, monsters, or anything else, they stand for the ghosts or spirits that frightened people on this same evening long ago.

Just as people once offered gifts of food to the spirits, people today offer treats to the children who represent them.

The lighted Jack-O'Lanterns the children carry are an echo of the fires and torches of former Halloweens and of the ancient Samhain.

The most sacred of Druid festivals, Samhain linked people with the dead and the past. It also expressed joy in the present and the life-giving harvest that ensured a future.

So children today, acting out remnants of ideas that people once lived by, link us with those who came before us and with those who will follow.

Stories for Halloween

BROCK, Emma L., et al. *Spooks and Spirits and Shadowy Shapes.* New York: E. P. Dutton & Co., Inc., 1949. A collection of pleasantly shivery stories for children of six to ten.

HARDENDORFF, Jeanne B., editor. *Witches, Wit and a Werewolf.* Philadelphia: J. B. Lippincott Co., 1971. Eighteen stories of ghosts, witches, and ghouls for children of nine to twelve.

HARPER, Wilhelmina, compiler. *Ghosts and Goblins.* New York: E. P. Dutton & Co., Inc., rev. ed., 1965. This edition includes several additional stories and poems, among them tales from Spain, Great Britain, and Japan, as well as poems by Carl Sandburg, Rowena Bennett, and Aileen Fisher. For children of seven and up.

HOPE-SIMPSON, Jacynth. *A Cavalcade of Witches.* New York: Henry Z. Walck, Inc., 1967. A large collection of poems and tales from all over the world and with a variety of interest levels, by such distinguished writers as Shakespeare, Burns, Yeats, C. S. Lewis, Walter de la Mare, and Mary Norton. There is an excellent introduction to each selection. This is a book for all ages.

MANNING-SANDERS, Ruth. *A Book of Ghosts and Goblins.* New York: E. P. Dutton & Co., Inc., 1969. Twenty-one stories from different lands, some funny, some hair-raising, retold by a distinguished writer. For children of seven to twelve.

NIC LEODHAS, Sorche. *Ghosts Go Haunting.* New York: Holt, Rinehart & Winston, Inc., 1965. Sorche Nic Leodhas brings the wealth of her Scottish background to this notable collection for children of nine to eleven.

SECHRIST, Elizabeth H., editor. *Thirteen Ghostly Yarns.* Philadelphia: Macrae Smith Co., rev. ed., 1963. Stories with emphasis on the humorous rather than the gruesome, for children of eight and up.

Index